Black Bears And Cubs
In Valdez Alaska

Bob Benda

ISBN:1530372216
ISBN-13:978-1530372218

DEDICATION

Dedicated to readers who enjoy watching and
photographing wildlife.

CONTENTS

ACKNOWLEDGMENTS

To my wife JoAnn for her patience and editing skills.

Black bears are seen regularly along Dayville Road in Valdez, Alaska. Dayville Road ends at the entrance to the Alyeska Marine Oil Terminal. The PetroStar Refinery, the Solomon Gulch Hatchery, and the Solomon Gulch Hydroelectric facility are also on Dayville Road. The black bears feed in the summer and fall on salmon. The salmon are returning to spawn in the streams flowing into Port Valdez. This photo shows a mother black bear with her three cubs. She's picked up a pink salmon carcass for the cubs to eat.

The mother bear has a very heavy coat. The three cubs are eating pieces of salmon in the muddy area. They are first year cubs. They were born in the winter den last winter. They are probably five or six months old. They don't catch salmon at this age, but depend on the mother bear to nurse them and provide food. They will start catching fish in their second year. They will separate from the mother bear in the second year.

While I was taking pictures of mom and the three cubs a bus full of tourists stopped on the shoulder of the highway. All the tourists left the bus and started taking pictures of the bears. They made so much noise they scared the bears. The mother bear and the cubs started running toward the grass along the opposite shore.

The mother bear reached the grass. The cubs were running after her. You can see how muddy the area was they ran across. This picture shows how heavy her coat was.

The mother bear ran into the grass. The cubs ran after her. They went through the grass, ran up the side of the bank and went into the brush.

Another time I was watching to see if any bears were feeding on salmon in this stream. A female black bear and one cub came out of the woods by the head of the stream. You can see the cub coming down the slope.

The mother bear walked into the water looking for salmon. The cub came down from the slope and followed mom to the stream.

Mom caught a pink salmon and brought it to the shore. The cub is sitting behind the branch watching mom.

Mom and the cub finished eating the salmon. Mom was looking toward the road. Several vehicles stopped to watch the bears and take pictures. This is a popular place for people to watch bears. I have seen several black bears with cubs eating in this area at one time. They usually feed in different parts of the stream.

The mother bear and the cub walked across the stream to the opposite shore. Mom caught another pink salmon. The cub was eating pieces of salmon left on the ground.

Mom finished eating the salmon and laid down to rest. The cub was pushing on her leg with its nose.

The mother bear didn't seem like she wanted to move so the cub decided to walk up the slope into the woods. Cubs usually stay near the mother bear. She will protect them if other bears are in the area. Male black bears can be a danger to the cub if the male bear wants to mate with the female bear. I was surprised the cub left the mother bear.

It got more interesting as I watched the cub walk up the slope into the woods. The mother bear got up and walked another way. I thought it would follow the cub.

The mother bear walked over to another part of the stream and started to lay down. You can see the orange salmon eggs in the gravel by the log. There are also many salmon carcasses laying in the gravel.

The mother bear started licking up the salmon eggs from the gravel. All the bears I have watched and photographed seem to prefer the eggs if they can get them. They are expelled from a ripe (one ready to spawn) female when the bear catches the fish.

Now mom got up and caught another pink salmon to eat. The stream divides around this area and rejoins the main stream closer to the highway culvert. Salmon swim up both branches of the stream and spawn in the gravel.

She caught another ripe female pink salmon this time. As the mother bear bites the fish's abdomen you can see the orange eggs being expelled.

Mom finished eating the salmon and laid down to rest. I couldn't believe what I saw next. The cub came out of the woods and was walking down the branch above the mother bear.

The cub was hanging onto two branches trying to figure out how to get to the mother bear. Either she doesn't notice the cub or she is indifferent to its appearance.

The cub is now on one branch several feet above the mother bear. Mom doesn't seem to be too excited and isn't even looking at the cub.

   The cub must have decided to hang on the branch with its two front paws and try and reach the ground. Mom still isn't looking at the cub or trying to help it down.

The cub is now holding onto the branch with one paw. It's touching the mother bears head with its hind leg. She doesn't seem to notice.

The cub let go of the branch and dropped down to the ground. The mother bear looked up. She still has the salmon she caught under her paw. You can see the eggs by her paw. The cub dropped so fast I missed taking that picture.

The mother bear got up and walked back into the stream. She caught another salmon. While she was doing this the cub started walking back into the woods. It looked like it was leaving again.

The cub did leave the mom and went back into the woods. This was the first time I ever saw a black bear cub leave its mom. It left her not once, but two times to wander off into the woods. The mother bear walked back to the head of the stream and caught another salmon. She didn't seem concerned that the cub was gone again.

I watched the mother bear eat the salmon and then walk across the stream to the rocky slope. As she approached the slope the cub walked out of the woods and started walking down the slope towards her.

The cub met up with its mom at the bottom of the slope. The mother bear started walking up the slope. The cub turned around at the bottom of the slope and followed her.

Mom walked past the brush on the side of the slope. This slope was composed of rock brought down by a landslide early this spring. This stream's flow characteristics have been changed each year by slides like this.

In late summer I saw a mother black bear and three cubs coming out of the brush. They were by a waterfall along Dayville Road. I don't know if these were the same cubs on pages 1 to 5 at the beginning of this book. They could be since triplet cubs are not that common. This mother bear has a distinctive white V shaped mark on her chest. I never saw the other mom with the three cubs from the front to see if she had a V mark. All I can say is I assume these may be the same cubs.

Mom and the cubs walked over by the waterfall. She caught a salmon for them to eat. You can see the salmon swimming in the water and carcasses washed up on the rocks. This area is affected by the tidal changes. High tide washed the carcasses up on the shore.

The mother bear and two of the cubs start eating the pink salmon. The third cub is walking towards the waterfall.

The cub stopped when it found something else to eat. The mother black bear and the other two cubs continued eating the pink salmon.

The third cub is back with mom and the other cubs. Mom looks toward Dayville Road at the people taking pictures. She has a mouth full of salmon.

Here's mom and the cubs feeding by the waterfall. During summer both brown bears and black bears come here to feed on spawning salmon. In the fall bears come here to feed on the salmon carcasses. They will turn the carcasses over trying to find salmon eggs.

While the cubs finish eating the salmon the mother bear starts looking for another pink salmon to catch. When the bears are bothered by too many people taking their pictures they will catch a last salmon and go back into the woods.

Two of the cubs watch her as she catches another salmon. The third cub is looking the other way. It may know they are leaving this area.

The mother bear must have decided it was time to leave the waterfall area. She took the fish she caught and started walking back along the shore. The three cubs started to follow her.

Mom and the cubs reach the grass area along the shore. One cub is walking with mom while the other two cubs are following. Mom is carrying the salmon.

Mom and the cubs leave the grass area and enter the brush along the shore. She's taking the salmon she caught back into the woods. Mom and the cubs will share it later. Maybe it'll be a "Midnight Snack".

They are almost into the woods. They're done feeding for today. This is also the end of the three black bear stories in this book..

ALASKA BLACK BEAR FACTS

1. An estimated 100,000 black bears inhabit Alaska

2. Black bears vary in color from jet black to white. Black is the most common color, but brown or cinnamon-colored black bears are found in Alaska. Some bluish-colored black bears, called glacier bears are found in Southeast Alaska. Black bears often have a brown muzzle and some have a patch of white hair on their chests.

3. Black bears are the smallest of the North American bears. Adults stand about 29 inches (74 cm) at the shoulder and are about 60 inches (153 cm) from nose to tail. They weigh from 180 to up to 350 pounds (81 kg to 158 kg). They are 20 percent heavier in the fall than in the spring when they emerge from their winter sleep. Male black bears are larger than females. The 10th largest Boone and Crockett world record black bear was killed on Kuiu Island, Alaska in 1996.

4. Black bears occur over most of the forested areas of the state.

5. They may be found from sea level to alpine areas depending on the season of the year.

6. For most of the year black bears are solitary animals. They mate in June through July. Black bears mature sexually at 3 to 6 years of age. In southern Alaska black bears will breed every other year. In northern Alaska black bear females keep their cubs with them an extra year and will breed every third year.

7. One to four cubs may be born, but two is the most common. The cubs are born in the winter den following a gestation period

of about seven months. Cubs remain with their mothers through the first winter following birth.

8. Black bears are omnivorous, meaning they eat both plant and animal tissue. They are called creatures of opportunity and will eat anything they encounter. They eat freshly sprouted green vegetation in the spring, salmon in the summer, and berries in the fall.

9. Black bears spend the winter in a state of hibernation. Their body temperatures drop, their metabolic rate is reduced, and they sleep for long periods. Unlike true hibernators black bears in southern Alaska will emerge from their dens in winter.

Further information can be found at: www.adfg.alaska.gov/blackbear

ABOUT THE AUTHOR

Bob Benda is a retired Professor of Biology. He has taught at several colleges and universities during his career. He worked for two years in East Africa on a Lake Victoria fisheries project. He worked for the U.S. Fish and Wildlife Service and the U.S. Forest Service. He also worked for the Alaska Department of Environmental Conservation during the Exxon Valdez oil spill. He participated in oil spill damage assessment studies for the University of Alaska after the oil spill cleanup.